I0529923

# Brave Money
## Build Financial Freedom, Confidence, and Wealth as a Single Mom, Without Shame, Guilt, or Fear
## Sefi Wells

Novane Publishing, LLC

# Copyright

# Contents

**For every woman who ever wondered if she was strong enough to start over.**

For the mothers building futures from broken pieces. For the dreamers raising their children and themselves at the same time. For the ones who dared to believe that financial freedom was for them, too.

You are not just surviving. You are building legacies.

This is for you.

Let's keep building.

# Introduction: You are Not Broken

## Reclaiming Your Power Over Money

You're here because you're tired. Tired of feeling like no matter how hard you work, how much you stretch, or how deeply you sacrifice, it's never quite enough. Tired of the late-night worry that creeps in like an unwelcome shadow, whispering questions that have no easy answers. Tired of carrying the crushing weight of responsibility for a family you love more than life itself, while wondering if you're doing it "right."

If any of that sounds familiar, let me say this loud and clear: **You are not broken.**

Financial struggle has a way of making even the strongest among us feel small. It chips away at your confidence. It plants seeds of shame that grow wild if left unchecked. It convinces you that your stress is a personal failing, not a symptom of a system that demands everything and gives very little in return.

You are not here because you made "bad choices." You are not here because you are lazy, irresponsible, or destined to struggle. You are here because you are ready for something more, for yourself and for your children.

This book was written for women like you: women who are doing it all, often alone, often unseen, and who deserve tools that respect the depth of their journey. Not just surface advice about budgeting. Not just hollow cheer-leading about "manifesting abundance." You deserve a path that honors both your reality and your dreams.

In these pages, you will find more than just financial strategies. You will find healing. You will find empowerment. You will find a blueprint built for real life, not some fantasy world where everything goes perfectly and no child ever spills milk all over an important bill.

We'll start by addressing the real emotional weight that money carries, the fear, the shame, the exhaustion that no spreadsheet can fix. Then, step by step, we'll build practical systems that move you from panic to stability, from survival to security, from feeling stuck to creating freedom.

You'll learn how to:

- Build an emergency fund, even when every dollar already feels spoken for.

- Break free from the cycle of debt without adding more stress.

- Create a spending plan that supports your dreams instead of punishing your hopes.

- Increase your income in ways that respect your energy and time.

- Start investing, even if right now that word feels intimidating.

- Teach your children a new legacy of confidence, stability, and wisdom around money.

Most importantly, you'll learn how to stop letting money define your worth.

I won't promise you overnight miracles. Real change rarely happens that way. But what I will promise you is a journey of small, steady, courageous steps. And I'll be here, walking alongside you through each one.

You are capable of incredible things. Not because you must be "superwoman" or do everything perfectly. But because resilience is already in your DNA. You have survived every hard day you've faced. Now, it's time to build a life where you don't just survive, you thrive.

This is more than a money makeover. This is a reclaiming of your power, your peace, and your future.

Let's begin.

# Facing the Fear
## Why Money Feels So Overwhelming

If you've ever found yourself lying awake at night, heart racing over a missed bill or wondering how you'll stretch what's left in your account until payday, you are not alone. For many single mothers, financial fear isn't just an occasional visitor, it's a constant companion, an invisible weight that makes even simple choices feel overwhelming. It's not just about struggling to pay bills. It's about feeling trapped in a cycle of fear, with no easy way out.

But here's the truth that often gets buried under layers of shame and exhaustion: your fear around money is not a sign of weakness. It's not because you're bad with finances. And it certainly doesn't mean you're failing.

Money fear runs deep because it's tied to something much bigger than dollars and cents. It taps into our most primal need for safety, security, and survival. When the rent is due, when groceries run low, when a child's needs clash with an empty wallet, it triggers a very real and very human fear: "Will we be okay?" That fear isn't just rational, it's biological. Your body and mind are reacting exactly as they were built to when stability feels threatened.

For single mothers, this fear often wears extra layers. Maybe you've been told by society, family, or even yourself that you should "have it all together." Maybe you've absorbed the cruel idea that struggling financially means you're irresponsible, lazy, or somehow not good enough. That's a lie. The reality is that you're doing the work of two (or more) people with half the resources, often while carrying the emotional weight of worry, guilt, and pressure.

Understanding why money feels so overwhelming is the first step to reclaiming your power. It's not just about "getting better at money." It's about healing the emotional wounds that make every financial decision feel like life or death. It's about rewriting the story that says struggle defines your worth.

Maybe growing up, you saw adults around you stressed about money, fighting over it, or making it seem like something too complicated to ever master. Maybe you watched caregivers silently suffer through financial hardship, modeling a pattern of fear and silence around money. Those experiences sink in. They teach us, often without a word being spoken, that money is something dangerous, elusive, or shameful.

And when you became a mother, that fear only deepened. Now, every dollar feels tied to your child's well-being, to their dreams, to their future. The stakes are higher. The pressure is heavier. Suddenly, it's not just your survival on the line, it's theirs too.

So if money feels overwhelming, it's not because you're broken. It's because you care. It's because you're trying, day after day, to hold up a world by yourself. That takes courage beyond measure.

Here's the even better news: you won't have to climb mountains overnight. You'll take small, steady steps, each one a victory against fear, and together, we will build the life you deserve.

In this chapter, I don't want to offer you a band-aid. I want to offer you a mirror, one that reflects the truth that's been hidden by fear: You are already powerful. You have survived 100% of your hardest days. And money, while important, does not get to dictate your worth.

The path to financial empowerment doesn't start with calculators or budgets, those come later. It starts here, in the quiet, courageous decision to stop running from the fear and start facing it with open eyes and an open heart. Because once you understand that fear is just a messenger, a signal that you're ready for something better, you can start listening to it without letting it control you.

You don't need to "conquer" your fear. You don't need to be fearless. You just need to walk forward anyway.

This book will walk with you every step of the way, showing you how to move from panic to peace, from survival to security, and finally, to freedom. You're not here to survive fear forever. You're here to outgrow it.

You are not stuck. You are not powerless. You are already rising.

Let's keep building.

# Emergency Readiness

## Building Your First Financial Safety Net

P icture for a moment, a life where one unexpected expense, a flat tire, an unanticipated school fee, or a sudden doctor's visit, doesn't send your heart plummeting into your stomach. Envision the peace of mind that comes from knowing that when life throws its inevitable curve-balls, you have a small but mighty cushion ready to catch you.

Imagine standing at the auto shop and calmly handing over your debit card for a repair. Imagine facing an unexpected school fee and, instead of scrambling or panicking, calmly transferring money from your security fund without hesitation, no borrowing, no dread, just steady, prepared action. That's the kind of power even a small emergency fund can bring.

An emergency fund offers **peace, not perfection.**

Too often, emergency funds are talked about as if they're some far-off luxury, something only "rich" people build once they've already "made it." But the truth is, **you deserve that safety net right now**, exactly where you are.

Building an emergency fund isn't about instantly saving thousands of dollars; it's about creating a small but reliable cushion that offers immediate relief when life throws the unexpected at you. A well-placed emergency fund can turn a bad day into just a bump in the road, instead of allowing it to spiral into a bad month, a bad year, or a major setback that threatens your stability and confidence.

## Why Emergency Readiness Matters

Without a financial cushion, every surprise becomes a crisis. A minor emergency can quickly snowball into a life-altering disaster. Picture this: your car won't start on Monday morning. You find out the battery is dead, and the alternator needs replacing, a $300 repair. Without an emergency fund, you can't pay for the fix right away. That means missing three days of work, losing crucial income, and suddenly struggling to cover rent that's due at the end of the week. What started as a simple car issue has now snowballed into a full-blown financial crisis. Without a buffer, small emergencies grow into life-altering setbacks that feel almost impossible to recover from.

A small, or minor emergency, can spiral into missed work, missed paychecks, even lost housing. Without a backup, options like credit cards, payday loans, or family "favors" can start to feel like the only way out. But each comes with heavy hidden costs. Credit cards often carry high interest rates, meaning a $300 emergency can turn into $500 or more over time if not paid off quickly. Payday loans, while tempting for their fast cash, can trap you in a cycle of debt with astronomical fees and interest rates that can top 300% annually. Even borrowing from family, while seemingly harmless, can create emotional strain, feelings of guilt, and complicated power dynamics that linger long after the money is repaid. Financial emergencies without a cushion don't just drain your bank account, they can drain your hope, your relationships, and your emotional strength.

An emergency fund changes the game. It allows you to breathe. It lets you meet life's challenges from a place of strength, not fear. It doesn't erase hardship, but it **empowers you to handle hardship without losing your footing**.

This is about survival first. Security second. Freedom third.

And we start by focusing on a very attainable first goal: **saving $500.**

## Why $500?

Because, $500 might not sound like a fortune, but it's powerful enough to change everything. It's enough to cover the kinds of emergencies that often throw households off track, like paying for that sudden car repair, covering a surprise utility bill when the heater breaks down in winter, or handling a medical co-pay after an unexpected trip to the urgent care. It's a number that's big enough to offer real protection but small enough to feel achievable, even when money is tight. Reaching $500 moves you out of that terrifying space where "one bad day" could completely derail your stability. It gives you breathing room, the chance to make decisions calmly, and the strength to weather life's storms without slipping backward.

When you reach your first $500, you won't just feel "a little better." You will feel **different**. Stronger. More prepared. Less trapped.

## How to Start Building Your Safety Net

You don't have to save $500 all at once. You just have to start.

Here are some practical, realistic steps to create your first safety net:

**1. Open a Separate Emergency Savings Account** Find a free, no-minimum savings account, preferably at a different bank from your checking account to avoid "accidental" spending. Label it something powerful like "Security Fund" or "Peace Fund."

**2. Save the "Unexpected Extras"** Tax refunds, birthday money, overtime pay, even small windfalls. Instead of letting them disappear, funnel them into your emergency fund. Unexpected money deserves an unexpected future.

**3. Cut One Small Thing Temporarily** This isn't about cutting joy forever. But temporarily pausing one recurring expense, a subscription, a drive-thru meal habit, can free up $10, $20, $30 a month toward your goal.

**4. Sell Something You Don't Need** That old stroller, the secondhand dresser you've been meaning to replace, unused gadgets, turn clutter into security. One $50 sale is one big step closer.

**5. Side Hustle for a Sprint, Not a Marathon** Pick up one small, short-term gig, babysitting, freelancing, dog-walking, just to build your fund. Then stop. Sprinting temporarily is very different from signing up for long-term exhaustion.

**6. Set an Automatic Transfer** Even $5 a week, set on autopilot, adds up. Automatic savings turns good intentions into guaranteed action.

### 7. Round Up Your Purchases

Use apps that automatically round up each purchase to the nearest dollar and deposit the change into savings. It's painless, and it adds up faster than you think.

### 8. Pocket the Found Money

Every time you find loose change, rebate checks, or small refunds, treat it like treasure and move it straight to your emergency fund. Every penny is another knot in your safety net.

## Emotional Shifts That Matter

Building your safety net isn't just a financial task. It's an emotional revolution.

Every dollar you save is a statement: **"I am securing my future. I am building peace for myself and my children. I am not powerless."**

Saving your first $500 is not "small." It's massive. Because it rewrites the story you tell yourself every time an unexpected bill arrives. Instead of fear, you get to feel readiness. Instead of panic, you feel pride.

Every time you add even a few dollars, celebrate it. You are laying bricks of security that no one can take away from you.

## If You Feel Overwhelmed, Remember This

You don't have to be perfect.

Give yourself full permission to have imperfect weeks. Some seasons will be heavier than others. Missing a savings goal doesn't erase your progress. It doesn't define your worth. It simply means you're human, and you are still winning by refusing to give up. You don't have to do it fast. You just have to **keep moving forward.**

Some weeks, you might be able to tuck away $5. Other weeks, saving anything at all might feel completely out of reach. That doesn't mean you're failing, it means you're living real life. Building your safety net isn't about being perfect every week. It's about the decision to keep moving forward, even when the steps feel small. This isn't a race. It's a quiet, steady rebellion against the cycle of fear that has already taken too much from you.

With every dollar you save, you are rewriting the story. You are building a future where surprise expenses don't have the power to tear apart your peace of mind. You are strengthening yourself, one brave and beautiful step at a time.

Let's keep building.

# Slaying Debt Shame
## The Truth About Getting Free

D ebt is a heavy word. It carries not just financial weight, but emotional baggage too. For many single mothers, debt feels like an invisible chain, wrapping tighter around your dreams with every missed payment, every new bill, every moment you wonder how you'll ever get ahead.

You might notice it first in your tight shoulders, in the way you lie awake at night worrying, or in how hard it becomes to smile genuinely. Debt isn't just a financial burden you carry in your wallet; it's a heavy weight that presses down on your spirit, affecting every part of your life.

But here's what most books and "experts" won't tell you: **debt is not a moral failing.**

Debt is a tool, one that, like any tool, can be used well, used poorly, or used out of necessity in moments of survival. It may sometimes be a stepping stone and other times a stumbling block, but it is never, not once, an accurate reflection of your worth, your intelligence, or your ability to build a better future.

That's why the first step toward freedom is clearing away the shame that debt tries to pile on. Shame is the heavy fog that clouds your thinking and convinces you that you're bad with money, irresponsible, or too far gone to turn things around. But shame isn't telling you the truth. It's telling you a story designed to keep you stuck. And it's time to write a better one.

Most debt happens because people are trying to survive. Medical bills. Car repairs. Groceries when the paycheck didn't stretch far enough. Student loans taken out with hope for a better life. Credit cards used to bridge impossible gaps.

**Debt is often the result of courage, not failure.** It's the mark of someone who kept going when the world didn't offer easy options.

Think about the mother who used a credit card to buy groceries because her children needed to eat that night. Or the woman who paid for a necessary car repair with borrowed money because missing a week of work wasn't an option. These are not stories of failure. These are stories of love, survival, and strength under impossible pressure.

Now, with that shame out of the way, we can focus on what matters: **freedom.**

You deserve to be free from the constant anxiety of owing others. You deserve the peace of opening your mail without dread. And you can get there, not by beating yourself up, but by taking steady, strategic steps forward.

## Step 1: Know Your Numbers Without Fear

This can feel scary, but knowledge is power. Make a list of every debt you owe: balances, minimum payments, and interest rates. Breathe through it. You are gathering information, not judgment.

Imagine you're a mechanic inspecting a car, you're just assessing what needs attention. You are not the problem. Debt is a problem that can be fixed.

## Step 2: Prioritize Your Debts

Start by focusing on either:

- **Smallest Balance First (Snowball Method):** Paying off little debts first gives you quick wins and builds momentum.

- **Highest Interest Rate First (Avalanche Method):**
  Paying off high-interest debts saves you more money in
  the long run.

Pick the method that feels most motivating for you. There's no "perfect" choice. Forward movement is what matters.

## Step 3: Protect Your Energy and Resources

When creditors start calling, it can feel overwhelming and invasive. But it's important to remember that you have rights, and you are not powerless in these situations. You have the right to request that creditors communicate with you only in writing, giving you space to respond thoughtfully instead of reacting under pressure. You also have the right to negotiate payment plans that fit your reality, not theirs. And if navigating these conversations feels too heavy, you can seek support from nonprofit credit counselors who exist to advocate for you, not to profit off your situation.

You are not obligated to answer every call. You are not required to absorb verbal threats or intimidation tactics. Protecting your mental health is just as important as protecting your financial health. Setting clear boundaries during this process isn't just allowed, it's a vital part of reclaiming your power.

## Step 4: Celebrate Every Win

Paying off a $50 balance might seem small when you compare it to a $5,000 loan, but make no mistake: every debt you eliminate is a weight lifted from your back. Every payment is a tangible act of reclaiming your future. Each step forward is an act of quiet rebellion against the hopelessness that debt tries to create inside you.

To keep your momentum strong, consider starting a "freedom tracker." This could be a simple chart, a colorful notebook, a wall of sticky notes, anything that allows you to see your victories build up. Watching your progress take shape right before your eyes reinforces the truth that every effort matters. It turns invisible progress into something you can touch, celebrate, and believe in. Every stone you lift brings you closer to walking freely and proudly into the life you're building.

## Step 5: Forgive Yourself, Again and Again

You will have setbacks. An unexpected expense might slow your progress. A bad month might force you to skip an extra payment. That does not erase your efforts. That does not define your future.

This journey isn't about being perfect. It's about being persistent.

Debt freedom is not a one-day event. It's a season of rebuilding, just like healing a broken bone or planting a new garden. Some days you will sprint. Some days you will crawl. Both are progress. Both are worthy. Trust the slow, steady unfolding of your own comeback story.

## Emotional Shifts That Matter

Getting free from debt is not just about numbers. It's about reclaiming your belief in your future. It's about telling a new story where you are not buried by past choices but building new possibilities with every payment.

When you pay off a debt, no matter how small, you are telling the world, and yourself, "I am powerful. I am capable. I am free."

You are not the sum of your debts. You are the sum of your dreams, your courage, and your unstoppable resilience.

You are not the mistakes you made. You are the strength that kept choosing to rise anyway.

This chapter is not the end of your fight against fear. It's the beginning of your walk into freedom. And every brave step you take, every dollar you reclaim, brings you closer to a life where money no longer chains you, but lifts you.

You've already survived so much.

Let's keep building.

# Money Mapping

## Building a Budget That Feels Like Freedom

B udgeting. Just the word alone can bring a wave of dread.

For many single mothers, the idea of sitting down with a spreadsheet feels about as appealing as going to the dentist, necessary, maybe, but anxiety-inducing at best. Traditional budgeting often sounds like endless "no's" and "cant's." It feels rigid, restrictive, and frankly, exhausting.

But here's the truth: **a real budget is not a punishment. A real budget is a map to freedom.**

It's not about squeezing every drop of joy out of your life to "prove" you're responsible. A restrictive budget feels like walking a tightrope, terrified of slipping with every step. A Freedom Budget feels like building a bridge, solid, steady, and designed to carry you safely toward the life you deserve. It's about giving yourself clear choices. It's about making sure the life you're working so hard to build actually reflects your dreams, not just your bills.

## Why Traditional Budgets Fail

Maybe you've tried a traditional budget before. You wrote it all down, color-coded every category, swore this time would be different. And then life happened: a child got sick, the car broke down, the utility bill spiked. Suddenly, the numbers didn't add up anymore, and instead of feeling supported, you felt like you failed. Not because you did anything wrong, but because rigid budgets don't live in the real world you live in.

Traditional budgets often fail single mothers for three major reasons:

1. **They don't account for chaos.** Life as a solo parent is unpredictable. Kids get sick. Jobs change. Expenses pop up out of nowhere. Rigid budgets shatter easily.

2. **They focus on guilt.** Most budget advice shames you for buying coffee, streaming shows, or taking your kids for a drive-thru treat. That shame fuels rebellion, not empowerment.

3. **They ignore emotional needs.** Money isn't just math. It's energy. It's emotion. A budget that feels like

a straitjacket will eventually get ripped off.

You need a different kind of plan, one built with **flexibility, forgiveness, and freedom**.

## Introducing the Freedom Budget

The Freedom Budget is designed for real life. It's not a diet for your dollars; it's a **roadmap to your dreams.** A Freedom Budget acknowledges your humanity by allowing room for real life to happen. It flexes when unexpected expenses arise and expands as your income, goals, and dreams grow alongside you.

Here's how to build it:

## Step 1: Know Your Baseline

First, list the essentials that absolutely must be covered every month (Your list may vary):

- Housing (rent/mortgage)

- Utilities

- Childcare/school costs

- Groceries

- Transportation

- Insurance

- Minimum debt payments

These are your *non-negotiables,* the pillars holding up your daily life.

## Step 2: Prioritize Your Peace

Next, add categories that protect your emotional and mental well-being:

- Emergency fund contributions

- Health and wellness (therapy, gym, self-care)

- Joy spending (yes, JOY spending!)

Even if you can only set aside $5 for "joy" right now, do it. Joy is not optional. It's fuel for the marathon you're running.

## Step 3: Plan for the Known Unknowns

Set up a "life happens" buffer category. Maybe $25/month. Maybe $10. Something small but sacred.

Because unexpected expenses are a part of life, whether it's a flat tire that needs repair, a last-minute school field trip with a fee, or suddenly outgrowing shoes overnight. Setting aside even a small monthly buffer gives you breathing room, turning what could have been a financial disaster into just another manageable part of your journey.

## Step 4: Give Every Dollar a Job

This is the heart of the Freedom Budget. Every dollar you bring in gets a purpose, even if that purpose is "cover next month's groceries."

Budgeting isn't about depriving yourself or living with constant restriction, it's about making intentional choices that align with your dreams. When money sits without direction, it tends to slip through your fingers on things that don't truly matter to you. But when you give every dollar a job, whether that's saving for an emergency fund, investing in your child's future, or simply protecting your peace, you turn your money into a powerful tool for building the life you envision.

## Step 5: Review Without Judgment

Choose a regular time that fits your life, maybe once a week, or twice a month, to sit down and review your budget. Take a few minutes to look honestly at your spending, see where things went right, and adjust gently where they didn't. Celebrate every win you notice, whether it's sticking to your grocery budget, saying no to an unnecessary expense, or simply staying aware of your choices. Small celebrations keep the momentum alive.

If you blow the budget? That's not failure. That's feedback. Learn, adjust, and move forward.

Budgeting is a practice, not a performance.

Remember: your Freedom Budget isn't carved in stone. It's a living, breathing map that changes as your life grows. Some months will demand more flexibility. Some seasons will require new priorities. That's not failure, it's wisdom. Adjust your budget as often as you need to. It's not about staying perfectly "on track." It's about making sure your money stays in service to the life you're building.

## Emotional Shifts That Matter

When you start mapping your money with care and intention, it changes more than just your bank account; it shifts how you see yourself. You stop feeling caught off guard every time you check your balance. You begin to feel proud of the choices you're making, even when they're hard. You let go of the chaos and start embracing clarity. And most importantly, you begin to believe that financial peace isn't a dream for "other" people. It's possible for you, too.

Your Freedom Budget isn't about rigid rules or constant sacrifice. It's a love letter to your future self. It says, "I trust the life I'm building. I believe in my ability to make decisions that reflect my dreams, not just my worries. I'm choosing a path where stress doesn't get to steer the wheel."

This isn't about tracking every penny down to the last cent. It's about finding a rhythm that works for your life. It's about using your money with intention, to support your goals, fuel your peace, and move you steadily toward the future you deserve.

If budgeting has felt like failure in the past, know this: you were never the problem. The system just wasn't built for your reality. But this one is.

You're not waiting for your future to magically appear. You're creating it, step by step, with every intentional choice you make.

And now, you've got a map to guide you.

Let's keep building.

# Income Power Moves
## Earning More Without Burning Out

I f you've ever caught yourself thinking, "It's not that I don't earn enough; it's that I'm already stretched to the edge of my time and energy," you are absolutely right.

As a single mother, you're already putting in more work than most people ever see. You're managing appointments, wiping away tears, packing lunches, helping with homework, handling crises, stretching every dollar, and keeping your family's world spinning, all while pouring every ounce of love you have into it. You don't lack work ethic. You're not lazy. You're tired, because you've been carrying more than your share for a long time.

So when we talk about earning more, we're not talking about hustling yourself into the ground. We're talking about building smarter, strategic, and sustainable income moves, ways to grow your financial power while fiercely protecting your energy and your well-being.

Because the truth is: **cutting expenses can only go so far. Increasing income is where transformation happens.**

## Why Earning More Matters

Budgeting helps you manage what you have today, but growing your income changes the reality you live in. When you earn even an extra $100 a month, it's not just a little more money, it's breathing room. It's the ability to handle unexpected bills without panic. It's watching your savings grow faster and your debt shrink sooner. It's seeing your dreams move closer, one step at a time. Most importantly, it's the moment you break free from the exhausting cycle of "just getting by" and start building a future with real choices.

## Step 1: Redefine "Work"

Not every "job" needs to be a 9-5 commitment. Not every dollar needs to come from clocking in at someone else's dream.

Think of your skills, your passions, your experience, even things you take for granted, as valuable resources.

- Are you great with kids? Babysitting, tutoring, or organizing children's activities.

- Are you creative? Selling digital art, writing, crafting.

- Are you a natural organizer? Virtual assistant work, resume editing, data entry.

- Are you bilingual? Translation services, tutoring language learners.

Your skills are seeds. Planted wisely, they can grow income streams that fit your life instead of draining it.

And don't forget: the skills you use every day to manage your family, negotiating, organizing, comforting, planning, are powerful. Just because society doesn't put a paycheck on emotional labor doesn't mean it isn't valuable. You already have a skill set built for resilience, creativity, and leadership.

## Step 2: Choose Between Fast Cash and Foundation Building

Not every opportunity serves the same purpose.

- **Fast Cash (Short-Term Relief):** Food delivery, ride-share driving, pet sitting, babysitting.

- **Foundation Building (Long-Term Growth):** Freelancing, building an online store, launching a consulting service, investing in a certification that increases your primary income.

Both fast-cash opportunities and foundation-building ventures have a role to play in your financial journey. The key is choosing intentionally based on what you need right now, and what you dream of creating in the long run.

Picture this: after deciding you need a quick financial boost, you spend two weekends delivering food. It's not glamorous, but it fits into your life without derailing everything else you're juggling. At the end of those weekends, you've earned an extra $300. When an unexpected doctor's bill arrives, you don't reach for a credit card or spiral into panic. Instead, you pay the bill calmly with the money you earned and put to work in your emergency fund. No stress. No shame. Just pride in your resilience, and a deep, steady peace in knowing you had your own back.

Ask yourself:

***"Do I need a quick boost right now, or am I planting seeds for bigger stability later?"***

## Step 3: Protect Your Energy with Boundaries

You cannot afford burnout, emotionally, physically, or financially.

Choose income streams that respect your reality:

- Flexible hours

- Remote options when possible

- Low startup costs

- Minimal emotional strain

No paycheck is worth sacrificing your health or missing the precious moments with your children. If an opportunity demands so much of you, it drains your energy or pulls you away from what matters most. It's not a true opportunity, it's a cost you may not be able to afford. Trust yourself enough to say no to work that empties you, no matter how tempting the paycheck may seem.

## Step 4: Maximize Your Main Income

Sometimes the biggest power move isn't a side hustle, it's negotiating better pay where you already are.

- Document your achievements.

- Research average salaries for your role.

- Practice asking for raises with confidence.

A one-dollar raise might seem small when you first hear it, but over a full year, it adds up to around $2,000 extra in your pocket. That's not just spare change, that's a month of rent paid. That's a full safety net you didn't have before. Small increases in your income can make a real, powerful difference in the security and breathing room you're building for your future.

## Step 5: Automate Your Extra Income

When you start earning extra income, it can be incredibly tempting to immediately patch every financial gap you see, to upgrade things you've been doing without, or to catch up on every overdue expense all at once. But one of the most powerful things you can do is pause, take a breath, and intentionally direct your new income toward the goals that will secure your future. Before you spend a dime, set up a plan to automate where that money will go:

- 50% to debt freedom

- 30% to emergency savings

- 20% to joy spending

Adjust these percentages based on your needs. The point is to make sure your new income **builds your future** before it slips away into "catching up."

## Emotional Shifts That Matter

Building new income isn't just about dollars. It's about re-building belief in your own possibility.

Every time you earn an extra dollar with intention, you remind yourself:

*"I am not stuck. I am not powerless. I have options."*

You are not sentenced to a lifetime of scarcity. You are capable of designing new paths, no matter how rocky the starting point.

You don't have to hustle yourself into the ground. You don't have to prove your worth through endless sacrifice. You are already worthy. You are already enough.

Now, it's time to let your income reflect your power.

You are building not just a paycheck, but a future of choice, dignity, and peace.

You are not waiting for opportunity. You are cultivating it with your own hands.

Let's keep building.

# Protecting What Matters
## Smart Moves for Crisis-Proof Living

L ife has a way of throwing curve-balls when we least expect them. One minute everything feels manageable, and the next a medical bill, a car breakdown, or a family emergency knocks you sideways. As a single mother, you carry the full weight of "what if?" on your own shoulders, and that burden can feel overwhelming.

But here's the empowering truth: **you don't have to control every storm to build a stronger shelter.**

You have the power to prepare, even in small ways, so that life's inevitable surprises don't dismantle the stability you're working so hard to create. Protecting what matters isn't about living in fear. It's about living with confidence.

## Step 1: Prioritize the Essentials

When you're building a crisis-proof foundation, you start by protecting the absolute essentials:

- **Housing**: Keep a roof over your heads, no matter what.

- **Utilities**: Power, water, and heat are non-negotiable.

- **Food**: Consistent access to nutritious food fuels your family's strength.

- **Transportation**: Your ability to get to work, school, and necessities matters deeply.

- **Health**: Basic medical care and mental wellness support must be prioritized.

Knowing your "essential four" creates clarity during tough times. If a crisis hits, you'll immediately know where to focus your energy and resources.

## Step 2: Build Layers of Protection

Think of your financial life like an onion, layer by layer, each one adding more resilience.

- **Emergency Fund (First $500, then 1 month's ex-**

**penses)**: This is your first, best defense.

- **Insurance**: Health insurance, renter's insurance, and even basic life insurance protect your future against catastrophic loss.

- **Savings for Irregular Expenses**: Car repairs, school fees, holidays, small, regular savings toward these known "surprises" helps avoid crisis-mode spending.

- **Important Documents Folder**: Keep copies of birth certificates, insurance policies, IDs, medical records, and a list of emergency contacts in a safe, accessible place.

Each layer you add buys you more breathing room when life gets complicated.

Consider creating a small "grab-and-go" emergency bag with copies of your important documents, a few days' worth of essential medications, basic supplies, and emergency cash if possible. In a fire, evacuation, or unexpected move, having this ready can turn chaos into calm.

## Step 3: Create a Simple Crisis Plan

It's not paranoid to have a plan. It's powerful.

Picture it: you show up to work one morning, only to be told your hours are being cut starting next week. That familiar knot of panic rises in your chest. But instead of spiraling into fear, you take a deep breath and pull out the simple crisis plan you prepared ahead of time. You immediately see which bills need to be paid first to keep the essentials running. You remember there's a food pantry just a few blocks away if you need it. You call a trusted friend, not just for advice, but for the emotional support that reminds you you're not facing this alone. Instead of freezing in fear or spiraling into panic, you move forward with steady, deliberate action, grounded by your preparation, strengthened by your courage, and ready to face the storm with resilience. That's the power of preparing ahead of time.

Ask yourself:

- If I lost income tomorrow, what bills must be paid first?

- Who could I call for help in an emergency, even if just emotional support?

- What community resources exist nearby (food banks, utility assistance, free clinics)?

Write your answers. Keep them somewhere you can find quickly when stress is high. Crisis clouds thinking. A written plan cuts through panic.

## Step 4: Practice "Controlled Flexibility"

Flexibility doesn't mean living in chaos or abandoning all plans. It means having the strength to adjust when life throws you something unexpected, without losing your balance.

Picture this: your car breaks down one morning, completely derailing your commute. It's frustrating, stressful, and expensive, but because you prepared with a small emergency fund and a backup transportation plan like bus routes or a carpool buddy, the situation stays manageable. You shift gears, handle what needs handling, and keep moving forward without falling into financial free fall.

Controlled flexibility is about staying rooted even when the ground shifts underneath you. It's the power to bend without breaking. Controlled flexibility empowers you to adapt with grace.

## Step 5: Strengthen Your Support Network

You don't have to shoulder everything alone. Think of your support system as a safety net, woven together by people and communities who care about you. Maybe that looks like a friend you can trade babysitting duties with, a relative who always shows up when it counts, or an online group of fellow single moms who truly get it. Just knowing you're not isolated can lift a huge weight off your shoulders and help ease the emotional burden during tough times.

## Emotional Shifts That Matter

Preparing for emergencies is an act of **self-respect**, not self-doubt.

You are not "inviting" bad things to happen by getting ready. You are acknowledging that life happens to everyone, and you deserve to face it from a place of strength.

When you protect what matters, you aren't just bracing for the worst, you're building a future where every curve-ball doesn't have the power to knock you down.

You are building a life of **resilience**, **resourcefulness**, and **radiant courage**.

Your children are watching. They see you calmly adjust plans when something breaks. They watch you face setbacks with resourcefulness instead of fear. They learn, deep in their bones, that life's curve-balls are challenges, not defeats. And through your quiet, powerful preparations, they will learn that true strength isn't pretending crises don't happen, it's knowing you can survive and thrive through them.

You are becoming unshakeable.

Being unshakeable doesn't mean you never worry. It means you stand steady even when the winds howl. It means you make decisions with clarity when others freeze. It means you face uncertainty with courage anchored deep inside you, because you prepared, you trusted yourself, and you refused to give up.

And that's a superpower worth claiming.

Let's keep building.

# The Mindset of a Wealth Builder

B y now, you've started to take action. You've faced your fears. You've started protecting what matters. Maybe you've even begun to earn a little more, save a little more, or breathe a little easier.

But here's a powerful truth that will shape the rest of your financial journey: **Wealth starts in your mind long before it shows up in your bank account.**

Real wealth, the kind that builds generational security, peace, and pride, begins with how you think about yourself, your future, and your ability to grow. If you want lasting change, you must begin to see yourself not just as someone who's "trying to get by," but as someone who is **actively building wealth** with every wise decision you make.

Because you are.

## Step 1: Ditch the Scarcity Script

For so many single mothers, the money story starts with scarcity:

- "There's never enough."

- "I'll always struggle."

- "I'm just not good with money."

These beliefs may have been planted in childhood. Maybe you grew up watching the people around you stress, argue, or go silent when money came up. Maybe you were taught that having too little was normal and that having more was impossible.

But scarcity isn't your birthright. It's a script, one that can be rewritten.

Start replacing those old lines with new truths:

- "I am learning how to create more than enough."

- "I am building better, for myself and my family."

- "Money is a tool, and I am learning how to use it with power and purpose."

Mindset isn't fluff. It's the frame that holds your future together.

## Step 2: Embrace a Growth Identity

You are not stuck where you started. You're evolving.

Picture this: you transfer $5 into your savings account and instead of brushing it off as "not enough," you smile and say, "I'm a woman who grows her future." One tiny celebration. One massive shift in who you believe you are becoming.

Wealth builders see every challenge as a step forward, not a stop sign. When something doesn't go as planned, they ask, "What can I learn from this?" instead of, "Why does this always happen to me?"

Adopting a growth identity means learning to recognize and celebrate even the smallest steps forward. Maybe you saved $10 this week; that's a win. Maybe you resisted the urge to buy something on impulse; that's real discipline. Or maybe you finally opened a savings account for the very first time, and that's a powerful beginning. Each of these actions, as small as they might seem in the moment, is evidence of you growing into someone who takes charge of their financial future. Every step builds confidence, and just like money, confidence grows with consistency.

## Step 3: Re-frame What Wealth Really Means

Wealth isn't just about big houses and luxury vacations. It's about options. Peace. Safety. Legacy.

Your version of wealth might look like:

- Being able to pay your bills on time every month without panic.

- Taking your kids on a trip without debt or guilt.

- Sleeping soundly knowing your future is secure.

When you define wealth on your own terms, you stop chasing other people's versions and start creating one that fits your life with pride.

## Step 4: Speak Wealth into Your World

The way you talk about money shapes how you feel about it, and how you believe in your ability to manage it. Words are powerful, and they can either reinforce fear or fuel growth.

When you catch yourself thinking, "I can't afford that," re-frame it by saying, "That's not in my plan right now." It reminds you that you're making an empowered choice, not living in lack.

Instead of labeling yourself with, "I'm broke," shift to, "I'm building." You are not stuck; you are in progress.

And when the old voice says, "I'm bad with money," replace it with, "I'm becoming financially strong." Because you are, every decision, every lesson, every brave step at a time.

Your language is your legacy in the making.

## Step 5: Surround Yourself with Wealth Builders

Your environment shapes your mindset. Surround yourself with people, books, podcasts, and voices that speak growth, not fear.

You deserve to be in rooms, physical or virtual, where financial empowerment is the norm, not the exception. Where women cheer each other on, share tools, and hold each other accountable.

If you don't have those people around you yet, that's okay. You're not alone, and you're not behind. Right now, let this book be your first reminder that you are capable of incredible growth. Let your own reflection be the first source of encouragement you see. Every powerful journey starts with believing in yourself, and as you move forward, the right people, the supportive voices, and the strong community you deserve will find you and grow around you.

Find mentors, voices, and communities that teach from a place of respect, not judgment. Look for people who understand that real wealth isn't built overnight or from picture-perfect circumstances. It's built late at night in cluttered kitchens, during quick breaks between double shifts, and in the quiet sacrifices no one else sees. Surround yourself with leaders who celebrate small wins, who honor the messy, brave middle of the journey, and who remind you, again and again, that your story is worthy of pride at every step.

## Emotional Shifts That Matter

This chapter isn't about wishful thinking. It's about reclaiming the narrative that says wealth is only for the lucky, the married, or the already comfortable.

You'll notice your mindset shifting when you pause before reaching for a credit card out of fear, or when you walk past a payday loan ad without feeling tempted. These small victories are proof: you are becoming the woman who builds, not the woman who breaks.

Wealth isn't some distant dream reserved for "someday" when life gets easier or quieter. It's not waiting for the kids to grow up or for everything to magically fall into place. Wealth, the freedom, security, and peace you've been working toward, is for you to begin building now, exactly where you are, with the resources and courage you already have.

Because wealth isn't only measured in money, it's measured in belief, in courage, and in the quiet decision to keep moving forward.

You are not your past. You are not your paycheck. You are not your mistakes.

**You are a wealth builder.**

Let's keep building.

# Mindset Traps

## How to Stop Comparison, Perfectionism, and Financial Self-Sabotage

You can have the smartest budget, the best side hustle, and a well-crafted plan for financial freedom, and still feel stuck if your mindset is pulling against you.

**Financial empowerment isn't just about managing dollars. It's about managing your thoughts.**

Many single mothers carry invisible battles within them, old fears, beliefs, and patterns that were built long before they ever had a chance to question them. If we don't bring these mindset traps into the light, they quietly keep us stuck, no matter how hard we work.

Today, we're going to name those traps, understand how they show up, and, most importantly, talk about how to set yourself free.

## The Silent Saboteurs: What's Really Holding You Back

It's not just the bills piling up, or the low-paying job that barely covers the basics, or the unexpected expenses that throw everything off track. It's the quiet, heavy voices that creep in when no one else is around, the ones that whisper, "You're too far behind to ever catch up," "You'll never figure this out," or "People like you don't get to build wealth."

Those voices aren't telling the truth. They're echoes of old fears and outdated beliefs, scripts you never chose, but that you're allowed to change. It's time to rewrite the story into one where you win.

### Real-Life Snapshot:

When Jasmine, a single mom of two, lost her job, it felt like the ground disappeared beneath her. Every time she scrolled through social media, it seemed like everyone else was thriving, landing promotions, buying homes, taking dream vacations. Compared to their highlight reels, her own life felt small and broken.

One afternoon, overwhelmed by it all, Jasmine made a different choice. She grabbed a notebook and started listing her small wins: the job applications she'd submitted, the tight grocery budget she stuck to even when it was hard, the way she reassured her kids that they would be okay, even when she wasn't sure herself.

It wasn't glamorous. No one posted congratulations. But it was resilience, steady, quiet, and powerful. Jasmine wasn't losing. She was laying the hidden bricks of a stronger future, one brave decision at a time.

## Mindset Trap #1: Comparison

Comparison drains energy you could be using to build your dreams. Social media makes it easy to feel like everyone else is winning while you're struggling just trying to keep your head above water. You see friends buying houses, going on vacations, posting about debt-free lives, and suddenly, your progress feels small and insignificant.

But here's the truth: social media is a highlight reel, not real life. Everyone's journey is unique, with different starting lines, obstacles, resources, and timelines. Comparing your journey to someone else's steals the energy you need to build your own.

Instead of asking yourself, "Why am I not there yet?" shift the question to, "How can I celebrate how far I've already come?" Every extra payment you make, every dollar you save, every boundary you protect, and every brave financial choice you make deserves recognition. These small wins aren't just steps, they are the building blocks of your future.

Remember, it's not about being perfect. It's about making steady, courageous progress. That's the real victory.

***Progress, not perfection, is the real victory.***

**Try a 3-Day Comparison Detox:**

For the next three days, give yourself permission to mute any social media accounts, emails, or even conversations that make you feel like you're not measuring up. Instead of spending 10 minutes scrolling, spend those minutes writing down a few things you're truly grateful for. At the end of the three days, check in with yourself: Has your mood shifted? Are you feeling a little more hopeful, a little more focused? Your energy is precious. Treat it like gold, because it is.

## Mindset Trap #2: Perfectionism

Perfectionism often whispers, "You have to get everything just right before you can even begin."

It convinces you to wait for the perfect timing, the perfect paycheck, or the flawless plan before taking that first step. But here's the truth: perfect doesn't exist. Waiting around for everything to line up just delays the growth you deserve. It's messy, imperfect action that actually builds momentum and changes your life.

You don't need a perfect plan to start investing. You don't need a flawless budget to begin saving. You don't have to be debt-free before you start dreaming bigger. You just have to start.

Real progress is messy. Healing is messy. Building a new, extraordinary future is messy.

And that's okay.

Give yourself permission to start right here, right now, even if it feels scary and imperfect.

**The Progress Over Perfection Pledge:**

"Today, I choose messy action over perfect hesitation. Today, I give myself permission to try, to learn, and to grow. Progress, not perfection, is my path to freedom."

Say it out loud. Write it down. Carry it with you when fear tries to freeze you.

## Mindset Trap #3: Self-Sabotage

Self-sabotage often slips in quietly, wrapped in the old stories you tell yourself, stories rooted in shame, fear, and the weight of past experiences. It whispers things like, "I'm bad with money," "I'll never be good at this," or "Who am I to believe I can be wealthy?"

It shows up in small, familiar ways: spending emotionally after a stressful day, avoiding checking your bank account because you're bracing for bad news, or giving up after a single setback because it feels like "this always happens."

But those moments aren't signs of failure. They're invitations, reminders that you're learning, growing, and building new, braver patterns, one choice at a time.

Self-sabotage feeds on shame and silence. It usually starts small, maybe an unexpected splurge after a hard day, or a bill you push aside, telling yourself you'll handle it later. Then shame creeps in, whispering, "See? You're terrible with money." That shame leads to avoidance: unopened bills, abandoned budgets, growing guilt. The longer it sits, the heavier it feels. It's not a character flaw, it's a painful cycle that keeps spinning until you interrupt it with compassion instead of criticism.

You don't break free by just trying harder or beating yourself up. You escape by meeting yourself with compassion instead of judgment. Real progress begins when you replace criticism with curiosity, when you pause and ask, "What can I learn from this?" instead of, "What's wrong with me?"

**How to break the cycle:** Talk to yourself like you would talk to a dear friend. When you slip, respond with curiosity, not cruelty. Remind yourself: a mistake is not a life sentence. It's a moment.

## Quick Re-frames for Common Thought Traps:

Instead of thinking, "I'm terrible with money," tell yourself, "I'm learning new money skills every day."

Instead of thinking, "I always mess this up," remind yourself, "Every mistake teaches me something valuable."

Instead of thinking, "I'll never get ahead," affirm, "Small steps forward still move me closer to freedom."

Every time you choose self-compassion over self-criticism, you weaken the grip of sabotage. You are not doomed to repeat the past. You are building new patterns, one brave step at a time.

## Building a Mindset That Builds Your Future

Mindset isn't a one-time decision. It's a daily practice. And the more you practice, the stronger it grows.

Start simple:

- Each morning, write down one thing you're grateful for and one small action step for the day.

- Each evening, list three tiny wins you accomplished, no matter how small.

- Throughout the day, affirm: "I am building my future with every choice I make."

Other daily practices that build mental resilience include:

- **Gratitude Lists:** Focus on what is working, not just what's missing.

- **Progress Journals:** Track wins, no matter how tiny.

- **Self-Compassion Breaks:** When things go sideways, pause and speak kindly to yourself.

- **Future Visualization:** Spend a few minutes daily picturing your financially free future. Feel it.

**Write to Your Future Self:** Take five minutes to write a letter from the version of you who has already achieved financial freedom. What does she want you to know today? What fears can she reassure you about? Let her voice guide you through the hard days. You are already becoming her, step by brave step.

## Emotional Shifts That Matter

You are not broken because you've struggled with money. You are not too late to change your story. You are not beyond hope.

You are learning new skills, one step at a time. You are breaking cycles that were never meant to define you. You are rising, stronger and braver with each imperfect decision you make.

Your future won't be built in one giant, perfect leap. It will be crafted through thousands of small, courageous choices, including the decision to keep believing in yourself, even when it's hard.

Let's keep building.

# Investing 101
## Making Your Money Work for You

You've already done the heavy lifting, building a stronger, more stable life for yourself and your family. Now, it's time to take the next bold step: **learning how to grow wealth that keeps working for you, even when you're not clocking in.**

This is where real financial freedom begins, the kind that gives you options, peace of mind, and breathing room.

If the word "investing" makes you feel a little nervous, you're not alone. Maybe you've heard it's complicated, risky, or something only "rich" people do. Maybe you've avoided it because it felt out of reach, like something you had to earn the right to do later.

But here's the truth: you are ready now.

Investing isn't reserved for Wall Street insiders or lucky lottery winners. It's meant for you. It's for anyone who dreams of building a life where they aren't tied to every paycheck, where their time and energy aren't endlessly exchanged for dollars. It's for anyone who believes their future should be about more than just getting by; it should be about thriving, growing, and creating real freedom.

Let's make investing simple, human, and doable, because it is.

## Step 1: Understand Why Investing Matters

Saving money is a huge accomplishment, but it's only part of the story when it comes to building lasting wealth.

Even the hardest workers can find themselves feeling stuck if they rely on savings alone. As prices slowly creep up year after year, the money sitting in a basic savings account quietly loses its buying power. That's where investing comes in. It's the bridge that turns your hard work into lasting security.

When you invest, you give your money a job: growing faster than inflation, building real assets like retirement funds, home ownership, or business opportunities. It's not about gambling; it's about planting seeds that grow steadily over time.

Instead of working harder and harder for every dollar, you begin to experience a shift, and your dollars start working for you. Investing is how you move from simply surviving to truly thriving, and it happens while you're busy living your life, sleeping, raising your kids, and building your dreams.

## Step 2: Know the Basics

You don't need to become a stock market expert to start investing wisely. You just need to understand a few key ideas:

- **Stocks**: A stock represents a small piece of ownership in a company. When you buy a stock, you become a partial owner of that business. If the company grows and becomes more valuable, your stock can grow in value too. Stocks can also pay dividends, giving you a share of the company's profits.

- **Bonds**: Bonds are like loans you give to companies, cities, or governments. When you buy a bond, you are lending them money for a set amount of time. In return, they agree to pay you back with regular interest payments plus the full amount later. Bonds are usually seen as steadier, lower-risk investments compared to stocks.

- **Mutual Funds/Index Funds**: Mutual funds are investment funds that pool money from many people to buy a collection of stocks, bonds, or other assets. A professional manager decides where to invest the money. Mutual funds are a way to diversify your investments without picking individual stocks yourself, but they often come with higher fees than ETFs.

- **ETFs (Exchange-Traded Funds)**: ETFs are investment funds that group together lots of different stocks, bonds, or other assets into one single bundle you can buy. When you buy an ETF, you're instantly investing in many companies at once, without having to pick individual stocks. ETFs are designed to make investing easier, safer, and more affordable for regular people. They trade like stocks, meaning you can buy and sell them anytime the market is open.

- **Dividends:** Some companies share a portion of their profits with their shareholders by paying out dividends. When you own dividend-paying stocks, or ETFs that include them, you receive a small cash payment, usually every few months. Dividends are a way for companies to reward investors for holding their shares, offering you steady income alongside potential growth.

Imagine you're shopping at a farmers' market. Instead of putting all your money into one single apple and hoping it stays perfect, you fill your basket with a mix of fruits, apples, oranges, bananas. That way, if one piece of fruit spoils, you still have plenty of others left. Investing works the same way: by spreading your money across different companies and industries, you protect yourself. Even if one investment doesn't do well, your overall basket still holds value and keeps growing.

## Step 3: Start Where You Are

It's completely normal to feel nervous when you're thinking about investing. You might wonder, "What if I choose wrong?" or "What if I lose money?" or even, "Where do I begin?" Here's the truth: every great investor you've ever heard of started with those same doubts. Courage isn't the absence of fear, it's choosing to move forward with small, steady steps even when you're uncertain.

The beautiful part is, you don't need thousands of dollars to get started.

Today, beginner-friendly platforms like Acorns, Stash, and trusted firms like Fidelity and Vanguard make it possible to start investing with as little as $5, $20, or $50. Every small dollar you invest is more than just money. It's a vote of confidence in the future you're building.

One great place to start is with a **Roth IRA** (Individual Retirement Account), if you're eligible. Think of it like planting a tree for your future. You invest a little today, and it grows tax-free into something strong you can rely on during retirement. Every dollar you contribute isn't just saving for someday; it's actively building your freedom and security, one small step at a time.

## Step 4: Stay Simple and Consistent

You don't need to chase flashy stock tips or try to guess the perfect moment to invest. Most people who build real wealth don't do it overnight, they do it by showing up month after month, year after year, staying steady, and letting time and consistency work their magic.

A simple, powerful strategy:

- Invest a little bit every month (even $25 counts).

- Stick to diversified funds (like an S&P 500 Index Fund).

- Leave your investments alone to grow over time.

Investing is like planting a tree. You water it, protect it, and trust that with time, it will bear fruit.

## Step 5: Trust the Long Game

Markets naturally rise and fall, that's part of how they work. What matters most isn't the daily ups and downs; it's the long, steady climb over years and decades. Long-term, history shows us that patience wins.

So when fear creeps in, when the headlines scream uncertainty, take a breath and remind yourself:

**You're not investing in today's chaos. You're investing in your future strength.**

Patience builds real wealth. Patience builds peace.

Picture your future self, standing stronger and freer because you planted the seeds even when you were scared, even when it felt impossible. Investing isn't about "beating the market." It's about outlasting the fear that once tried to hold you back.

## Emotional Shifts That Matter

Starting to invest isn't just a financial decision. It's an emotional declaration:

*"I believe my future is worth building."*

Every time you invest, no matter how small the amount, you are refusing to let fear or scarcity dictate your destiny.

You are creating a future where money works for you, not the other way around.

You are planting seeds not just for yourself, but for the generations that will come after you. You are becoming the foundation your family can stand on.

And you are doing it bravely, one dollar at a time.

Let's keep building.

# Protecting Your Progress

## Setting Financial Boundaries Without Guilt

Y ou've fought too hard and come too far to let guilt pull apart the stability you've built.

Financial freedom isn't just about the money you earn or save, it's also about the life you fiercely protect. For many single mothers, one of the hardest parts of financial healing isn't just budgeting smarter or paying down debt. It's learning how to set boundaries with the people we love most.

Saying "no" can feel almost impossible when you've spent a lifetime being the fixer, the giver, the one who stretches a miracle out of thin air. But here's the truth you need to hold close:

**Protecting your financial progress is not selfish. It is sacred.**

When you say "no," you're not just guarding your bank account. You're protecting your peace, your dreams, and the future you're building, brick by deliberate, beautiful brick.

## The Guilt Trap: Why Saying "No" Hurts (and Why It Matters)

Maybe it's a family member who needs "just a little help" to get by. Maybe it's a friend who assumes you'll cover the tab "because you're doing better now." Maybe it's the pressure to buy your child everything you couldn't have growing up, even when it stretches your budget to the breaking point.

The guilt whispers: *If you really cared, you would find a way.*

But real love, real strength, and real care are not measured by how much money you give away. They are measured by how fiercely you protect the future you are building for yourself and your children.

When you say "no" to unnecessary financial drains, you are not turning your back on anyone. You are turning your face toward the future you fought so hard to create.

## Spotting Financial Leakage: Where Progress Slips Away

Sometimes, the leaks are obvious, like when you loan money you can't afford to lose, co-sign a loan out of guilt, or end up paying bills that were never really yours to begin with.

Other times, the leaks are quieter and harder to spot. Maybe it's buying extra "just because" gifts when you feel bad about saying no, saying yes to pricey outings you can't really afford, overextending yourself with school fundraisers, or dipping into your emergency fund to solve someone else's crisis.

No matter how small they seem in the moment, every one of those leaks quietly chips away at the freedom and stability you're working so hard to build.

It doesn't always look dramatic. It might be a "small" $20 to help someone out one week, then $50 another week, then "just" covering dinner when you weren't planning to. None of it feels catastrophic in the moment until you realize it's slowly pulling precious resources away from your future self.

**You deserve to protect every brick you've laid. Every dollar. Every ounce of peace.**

## Building Healthy Financial Boundaries

Setting boundaries doesn't mean shutting people out or closing your heart. It means drawing clear, caring lines that protect your well-being while still holding space for the people you love. It's about making sure your needs matter too, and building relationships rooted in mutual respect, not silent sacrifice.

Here's how to start:

- **Clarify Your Priorities:** Your emergency fund, your future goals, your children's security come first. Period.

- **Prepare Scripts Ahead of Time:** Know what you'll say when asked for money or favors that don't fit your plan.

- **Set Giving Budgets:** If you choose to give, decide in advance how much you can give without harming your own foundation. Stick to it.

**Remember:** Boundaries are not walls. They are gates. You control when and how they open.

## Saying No Without Guilt: Scripts That Honor You

It's completely normal to feel awkward when you start setting boundaries. That discomfort doesn't mean you're wrong, it means you're stepping into a new, stronger version of yourself.

You might feel a pang of guilt, a knot in your stomach, or a worry that saying "no" will make you seem uncaring. Those feelings aren't the truth; they're echoes of old habits, old expectations that no longer serve you. Every time you honor a boundary, you're honoring the hard work and sacrifices that got you here.

Standing firm may shake you at first, but that's what real bravery looks like, doing the hard thing anyway, because your future is worth it.

Some phrases you can lean on:

- "I'm not able to help financially right now, but I'm rooting for you."

- "My budget is committed elsewhere this month. I hope you understand."

- "I'm focusing on some big goals for my family, and I'm staying very strict with my finances."

You don't owe anyone long explanations, apologies, or guilt. A simple, clear "no" is a full sentence when necessary.

## Emotional Shifts That Matter

Each time you honor your financial boundaries, you send a powerful message to yourself and everyone around you that your dreams, your peace, and your future are worth protecting.

You have the right to build a life free from debt to others. You have the right to choose your peace, even if it makes others uncomfortable. You have the right to fiercely guard the freedom you've worked so hard to create.

Boundaries are not betrayals.

**They are acts of fierce love for the life you refuse to sacrifice any longer.**

Let's keep building.

# Side Hustle Smarter, Not Harder

## Creating Income Streams That Respect Your Energy

When you're building a new life, the temptation to hustle 24/7 can feel overwhelming. Every ad, every guru, every social media post screams: *Grind harder. Sleep when you're dead. Hustle your way to freedom.*

But here's the truth they don't tell you:

**You don't need to work yourself into the ground to build wealth.**

You need to work smarter, not harder. Especially as a single mother, your time, your energy, and your emotional bandwidth are precious resources. They deserve just as much protection and strategy as your bank account.

## The Hustle Myth: Why Grinding Harder Isn't the Answer

Hustle culture paints a dangerous picture, one where burnout is seen as a badge of honor, exhaustion is mistaken for proof of your value, and endless hustling is sold as the guaranteed path to success. But the truth is, wearing yourself thin isn't a measure of your strength; it's a warning sign that something needs to change.

In reality, endless hustle often leads to:

- Burnout and emotional collapse

- Neglected relationships and health

- Poor financial decisions made out of desperation

You are not building a busier life. You are building a better one. One that makes space for your joy, your rest, and your dreams.

**You don't need more hustle. You need more strategy.**

## Fast Cash vs. Energy-Resilient Income

There will be times when you need a quick boost of extra money to stay afloat, and that's completely okay. Quick cash can be a powerful tool when used wisely. But it's important to remember that short-term hustles are meant to help you bridge the gap, not become a permanent way of life. Fast cash should lift you toward stability, not keep you stuck in survival mode.

**Good short-term side hustles for immediate cash flow:**

- Freelance writing, editing, or virtual assistant work

- Childcare, pet sitting, or elder care services

- Selling crafts, baked goods, or gently used items locally

- Food delivery or ride-share services (if safe and manageable)

These options can help you stabilize when needed without long-term commitment.

Fast cash can absolutely save you in tough moments, like a life raft that gets you safely across rough waters. But it's not meant to be where you stay forever. Spending too long in survival hustles can quietly wear you down, leaving you exhausted and stuck instead of moving forward. Think of your side hustle as a bridge to better opportunities, not the destination itself. Build the raft you need to get across, but always keep your eyes on the bigger, stronger future you're meant to create.

**Real-Life Snapshot:**

Take Maria, a single mom who started tutoring local kids in math during weekends. She kept it low-stress, charging a fair rate, setting boundaries on her time, and eventually turned her weekend side hustle into an online course. Maria didn't burn herself out chasing extra dollars. She built something sustainable, one hour at a time.

**A Word of Caution:** Not every hustle that looks good on paper will feel good in your life. If a side hustle demands so much of your energy that you have nothing left for yourself or your family, it's not freedom, it's just a second trap. The right side hustle should stretch you just enough to grow, but never so far that you snap. Trust yourself to know the difference.

**Good long-term, energy-resilient income streams:**

- Creating and selling digital products (ebooks, templates, courses)

- Building a blog or YouTube channel around a skill or passion

- Renting out space (garage, parking, storage)

- Affiliate marketing for products you genuinely love and use

Long-term income options are about creating a future where your money continues to grow even when you're not constantly putting in more hours. These kinds of opportunities respect your energy, your time, and your bigger dreams.

**Ask yourself:** Is this side hustle helping me build a freer, fuller life, or is it just keeping me busier and more tired?

## Choosing the Right Side Hustle for You

Before committing, ask yourself:

- Does this hustle fit into my current schedule without creating chaos?

- Am I genuinely interested or skilled in this area?

- Is there a path for growth or passive income later?

- Does it align with my long-term goals and values?

When selecting a side hustle, it's important to:

- **Respect Your Bandwidth:** Choose something that fits your current season of life, not someone else's highlight reel.

- **Align with Future Goals:** Pick side hustles that can eventually lead to bigger dreams, not just survival income.

- **Test Before You Invest:** Start small. Validate the hustle before pouring in big money, energy, or time.

**You are allowed to choose hustles that nourish you, not just deplete you.**

## Boundaries in Hustling

Just like setting financial boundaries helps you protect your money, setting boundaries around your hustle protects your time, your energy, and your spirit. It's about making sure that your drive to build a better life doesn't come at the cost of the life you're working so hard to create.

### Side Hustle Red Flags: Knowing When It's Time to Step Away

Not every opportunity is worth your time. Watch for these red flags:

- A hustle that constantly pulls you away from your children

- A side gig that leaves you physically or emotionally

wrecked

- Work that feels misaligned with your values or long-term goals

It's better to grow steadily and keep your spirit strong than to chase fast success and lose yourself along the way.

If you find that a side hustle is draining your joy or pulling you away from the life you're trying to build, it's more than okay to pause. It's okay to change your mind. It's okay to walk away from something that no longer fits. Pivoting isn't a sign of failure, it's a sign of wisdom, resilience, and self-respect.

## Emotional Shifts That Matter

**You are not here to prove your worth through exhaustion.**

You are already worthy.

Every dollar you earn with intention is a building block for your future. Every "no" you say to hustle-for-hustle's-sake is an act of self-respect. Every small, strategic step forward is a revolution against the belief that you must sacrifice your health, your happiness, and your family to succeed.

You are not just making money. You are building freedom. You are planting seeds that will bloom long after today's work is done.

Let's keep building.

# Celebrating Your First Financial Wins

When you're focused on chasing big financial goals, it's easy to miss the smaller victories happening right under your nose.

**But here's a truth you need to hold on to:**

*Small wins aren't small at all.*

They're the building blocks of your future, the quiet proof that you are moving forward, even when progress feels slow or invisible. Each small step, each brave choice, is another stone laid in the foundation of the stronger, freer life you're creating.

**Celebrating your first financial wins isn't just nice. It's necessary.**

The act of celebrating your small financial wins does more than create a moment of happiness. It fundamentally changes the story you tell yourself about who you are. Every time you recognize your progress, you fuel your motivation with real evidence that you are moving forward. You slowly build a new identity, one rooted not in fear or survival, but in strength, growth, and agency. Even more importantly, celebrating your wins keeps hope alive on the hard days when progress feels invisible and the finish line feels too far away.

Today, let's slow down, breathe deeply, and honor the brave, deliberate steps you've already taken. You deserve to see and celebrate how far you've come.

## Why Celebrating Wins Matters

Most of us grew up thinking that only the "big" milestones deserved celebration, like paying off massive debts, buying a home, or hitting a six-figure net worth. Those were the moments that seemed to earn applause. But real, lasting change is built on so much more than just the headline moments.

The real magic of lasting transformation doesn't happen in a few big, dramatic moments. It's built in the countless small, brave choices you make every day. The quiet decisions, the ones no one claps for, the ones that feel invisible but keep moving you forward. Those are the true foundation of your future.

Each time you stop and celebrate a small win, you're not just marking a moment, you're rewiring your mind to expect progress and believe in your own strength. These small acknowledgments build emotional resilience, giving you a deep well of courage to draw from during harder seasons. Momentum doesn't come from giant leaps; it's built steadily, patiently, through faithful, everyday steps.

If you don't pause to celebrate along the way, progress can start to feel like an exhausting, never-ending race. But when you take time to honor your wins, big and small, the journey feels meaningful, joyful, and sustainable.

## What Counts as a Win?

The short answer?

Anything that nudges you forward, even just a little.

Maybe you opened your very first savings account. Maybe you sent $10 extra toward your debt this month. Maybe you said "no" to a purchase that would've thrown off your budget. Maybe you stuck to your grocery plan for a full week, or finally had that hard, honest conversation about money you used to avoid.

Each of these moments matters. Each one deserves to be noticed and celebrated.

The world might not throw you a parade for these victories, but you should. Every small, brave choice you make lays another brick in the life you're intentionally building.

Progress isn't only measured in grand, sweeping changes. True progress is built quietly, one small decision, one brave moment, one steady step at a time.

## How to Track and Honor Your Progress

One of the most powerful ways to keep momentum alive is to track your wins intentionally, and celebrate them regularly.

**Start with a Victory Journal.** This can be a simple notebook or digital file where you record every financial win, no matter how tiny. When doubt creeps in (and it will), you have proof that you are growing, adapting, and moving forward.

Here are some real-life examples to spark your journal:

- "Transferred $5 to my savings account even though money was tight."

- "Said no to a lunch invite I couldn't afford without guilt."

- "Researched local credit unions to open a better savings account."

- "Talked to my kids about budgeting without shame."

Every choice you make, even the ones no one else sees, adds another brushstroke to the masterpiece of the life you're creating.

**Create a Financial Milestone Board.** You can use a coloring sheet, a sticky note wall, or a simple progress chart. The goal is to make your achievements visible. Each time you hit a savings goal, pay off a bill, or build a new habit, mark it proudly.

Seeing your progress with your own eyes builds emotional momentum in ways numbers alone cannot.

**Develop Tiny Celebration Rituals.**

Celebrating your wins doesn't have to mean throwing a big party or spending a lot of money. What matters is the intention behind it. Maybe it's lighting a candle to honor the moment, dancing around your kitchen to your favorite song, writing a quick love note to yourself, or treating yourself to a small, planned indulgence that fits your budget.

There are so many free ways to celebrate: blast your favorite playlist and dance it out, take a joyful walk around the block, text yourself a message of pride, or share your success with a friend who truly gets it and cheers you on.

Celebrating isn't about spending, it's about recognizing your strength, honoring your journey, and letting yourself feel proud of every step you've taken.

## Building Positive Emotional Momentum

Momentum isn't magic. It's something you consciously create by choosing to honor every step of progress, no matter how small. It's not found in grand gestures, but in the quiet daily decision to keep believing in yourself.

When you take the time to celebrate your small wins, you send a powerful message to your brain: **"This matters. Keep going."** You aren't just marking progress, you are reinforcing your identity as someone who builds, someone who honors growth, someone who refuses to give up.

Each celebration acts like kindling. One tiny spark of acknowledgment grows into a flame of self-trust. That flame, nurtured and protected, becomes a steady fire that fuels your future. Over time, your belief in yourself burns brighter than any obstacle in your path.

Momentum isn't something you stumble across or hope will magically appear. It's something you build, patiently, intentionally, through every small celebration, every brave choice, every ordinary day when you choose to keep going.

Don't wait until you hit the "big" milestones to feel proud. Pride belongs to you now, in every quiet step forward. It's not the opposite of humility; it's the living, breathing evidence that you are growing.

With every decision you honor, you're not just making progress, you're building resilience, belief, and a foundation of self-trust that will carry you through every chapter to come.

## Emotional Shifts That Matter

You are not "just surviving." You are not "barely scraping by." You are not "failing."

You are winning.

Every time you choose courage over comfort, even when fear feels louder, you win. Every time you draw a boundary to protect your financial peace, you win. Every time you invest, not just in your money, but in the woman you are becoming, you win. And every time you break even the smallest cycle of fear or scarcity, replacing it with hope, strength, and trust in yourself, you win.

Even if the world hasn't noticed your victories yet, trust that you are building something extraordinary. Even without applause, without headlines, without flashy milestones, you are planting seeds that will grow into something real and lasting.

Picture yourself, steady and strong, in your own quiet corner of the world, laying down brick after brick. You are building a foundation so solid that nothing and no one can take it away. Every brave financial choice you make, every new habit you honor, every whispered "keep going" you tell yourself, is living proof: you are transforming your life.

Brave Money isn't about chasing outside validation or waiting for someone to tell you that you've "made it." It's about learning to celebrate yourself, loudly, proudly, and without apology, right where you are.

You don't have to wait for a "perfect" moment, a big milestone, or the final goal to feel proud. You deserve to feel proud now, exactly where you stand.

Give yourself that permission.

Pride isn't arrogance. It's not selfishness. Pride is sacred. It's a deep honoring of the journey you've walked and the battles you've fought to stand here today.

You are not "bragging." You are not "getting ahead of yourself."

You are recognizing your own courage. You are honoring the woman you are becoming.

Pride is not the enemy of humility. Pride is the fuel that keeps your hope burning bright.

You are Brave Money in action.

And your story is only just beginning.

Let's keep building.

# Your First Brave Money Year

Congratulations, you've started something powerful.

Reading this book wasn't just a spark of hope; it was a bold commitment to yourself. Even if your voice trembled, even if you felt exhausted or uncertain, you made a promise: to believe in the future you are capable of building.

Now it's time to take that promise and weave it into the fabric of your everyday life.

**Your first year living Brave Money is a turning point.**

This is the year you take back the driver's seat of your life, no longer swept along by circumstances, but choosing, with intention, to lay strong foundations for lasting change. It's the year when those scattered hopes and half-starts finally turn into steady, grounded habits you can trust. It's the year you stop waiting for the "perfect" time to start and instead begin building right where you are, imperfectly, courageously, and beautifully.

In these next pages, we'll walk together through what your first Brave Money year can look like, and how you can move through it with resilience, clarity, and hope.

## Why the First Year Matters

In your first year, momentum matters far more than perfection.

This journey isn't about racing across every finish line as fast as you can. It's about creating steady new rhythms, new habits, new thought patterns, and new beliefs about what's possible for you.

You don't need to "win" every single month to create a year that changes your life. You just have to keep showing up, adjusting when needed, and staying committed to your vision.

Every tiny shift matters. Every dollar you choose to save, every time you check in with your budget, every time you pause to re-frame a negative mindset, it's all part of the larger masterpiece you're building.

Your first Brave Money year will teach you something powerful: you don't have to hustle your way to freedom. You can steady your way there, one imperfect, courageous step at a time.

## A Month-by-Month Brave Money Focus

Here's a simple map you can follow to create sustainable momentum without burnout.

### Months 1–3: Stabilize Your Base

- Build a mini emergency fund (even $500 makes a difference)

- Track your spending without judgment, just data gathering

- Set simple, clear financial goals for the next 12 months

### Months 4–6: Expand Your Capacity

- Explore side hustles or income-boosting options that fit your life

- Tweak your budget based on real data, not guilt

- Set a "tiny but mighty" monthly savings target (even $10 counts)

### Months 7–9: Strengthen Your Boundaries

- Practice saying "no" to money drains (unnecessary spending, emotional spending, guilt-based giving)

- Revisit your goals and celebrate progress (even tiny progress)

- Address one major financial fear or block with bravery

**Months 10–12: Reflect, Adjust, Celebrate**

- Audit your wins, no matter how small

- Adjust your goals based on what you've learned

- Plan one joyful, budgeted celebration of your growth

This plan isn't set in stone. It's a flexible, living guide designed to move with you, to adjust as your life shifts, your needs change, and your dreams evolve. You won't be forcing yourself to fit into a rigid structure; you'll be shaping your journey around the life you're actively building.

# Common First-Year Pitfalls (And How to Beat Them)

Everyone faces bumps in the road during their first Brave Money year. These are some of the most common challenges you might encounter, and more importantly, how you can move through them with strength and grace.

**Shame Spirals** Mistakes are going to happen. That's not a sign you've failed. It's proof that you're learning, growing, and doing the hard work of change.

**How to move through it:** Practice radical self-compassion. When you stumble, remind yourself: mistakes are detours, not dead ends. Pause, breathe, forgive yourself, and take the next small step forward.

**Comparison Traps** There will always be someone who looks like they have it all figured out. Especially in a world of perfectly curated social media feeds, it can be easy to feel like you're behind.

**How to move through it:** Stay rooted in your own journey. Your race, your pace. Your path is uniquely yours, and comparison only clouds the view of your own beautiful progress.

**Hustle Burnout** It can feel tempting to work harder and harder, thinking more hustle will speed everything up. But nonstop hustle isn't sustainable, it drains your energy and joy.

**How to move through it:** Prioritize rest and protect your energy as fiercely as you guard your income. Rest isn't a reward; it's a vital part of long-term success.

**All-or-Nothing Thinking** One bad spending day, one mistake, and suddenly it feels like all your progress is erased.

**How to move through it:** Remember: one slip doesn't cancel out months of effort. Reset without shame. One decision, one day, one choice at a time.

**Isolation** Choosing a different financial path from friends or family can sometimes feel lonely.

**How to move through it:** Find at least one person, a mentor, community, or accountability partner, who sees your vision and cheers you on. Courage multiplies when it's witnessed and celebrated.

You were never meant to build this life alone. Community makes the journey lighter, stronger, and infinitely more joyful.

## Create Your Brave Money Annual Ritual

Rituals are how we turn hopeful intentions into lasting habits. They give structure to change, transforming new behaviors into personal traditions that feel natural, sustainable, and deeply meaningful.

At the end of each Brave Money year, take time to:

- List your financial wins (no matter how tiny)

- Forgive yourself for any missteps

- Set 2–3 brave goals for the next year

- Write a letter to your future self celebrating the woman you're becoming.

**Guided Visualization:**

After your reflections, take a few deep breaths and close your eyes. Picture your future self standing confidently in the life you are working to build, peaceful, empowered, and secure. See her smiling with quiet pride, living the fruits of every brave step you're taking today. Feel the gratitude she holds for you, for daring to believe in her, for daring to keep going even when it was hard.

## Emotional Shifts That Matter

Throughout this journey, you are shifting from old patterns to new foundations. You are no longer waiting for permission to build wealth; you are claiming it. You are no longer letting fear drive your financial choices; you are choosing strategy and courage. You are no longer measuring success by speed; you are defining it by persistence and growth.

Every choice you make, every time you stay committed to your goals, every time you forgive yourself for a misstep, every time you celebrate a small win, you are building resilience. You are building agency. You are building a legacy that will ripple outward into your family and your future.

Every month you stay in the game is an act of rebellion against the voices that said it couldn't be done.

You are not fragile. You are not behind. You are not invisible.

You are a Brave Money woman, rising, building, and becoming.

And this first year? It's only the beginning.

Imagine the strength, the wealth, and the wisdom you will carry into the next ten years, all because you chose to believe in yourself today.

Let's keep building.

# Teaching Wealth to Your Children

There's a quiet, steady kind of power in realizing that the work you're doing today, the careful choices, the sacrifices, the brave steps forward, is not only changing your own life. It's reshaping the future for your children, too.

Each dollar you save, each boundary you honor, and each skill you build is like planting a seed in their lives. Those seeds will grow long after they step out into the world on their own.

You aren't just building wealth for yourself. You are laying down roots that will support generations to come.

**You are building a legacy.**

And you don't need to be a millionaire to teach your kids about money. You just need to teach them something many of us never learned growing up: that money is not something to fear, fight over, or worship. It's a tool, a powerful, empowering tool, they can learn to use with confidence.

## Step 1: Normalize Talking About Money

In many families, money wasn't something you talked about openly. It either simmered beneath the surface as a constant source of silent stress, or it exploded into loud arguments that left everyone feeling helpless. Money often felt mysterious, confusing, or even shameful, something you were supposed to worry about but never fully understand.

Break the silence in your home.

You don't need a perfect script. Everyday moments are opportunities: "Why do you think we're saving up before we buy a new car?" or "What would you save for if you had $20?" Simple questions open the door to confidence, curiosity, and connection.

Start simple:

- Talk about saving for goals.

- Explain what bills are in age-appropriate ways.

- Share wins: "Today I paid off a credit card!"

When money is treated like a normal, open subject, kids grow up seeing it as manageable, not scary.

## Step 2: Teach by Example

Children absorb lessons not only through lectures, but through the quiet, everyday examples they see. They watch how you handle money, how you save, how you spend, how you make decisions, and those actions leave lasting impressions that words alone rarely can.

When you budget, save, invest, or even say "no" to unnecessary spending, you are teaching them:

- Discipline is powerful.

- Planning is empowering.

- Saying "no" now can mean saying "yes" to bigger dreams later.

Your everyday actions become their lifelong lessons.

## Step 3: Involve Them in Age-Appropriate Ways

Even young children can start learning basic financial concepts:

- **Ages 3-6**: Play "store" games. Teach that things cost money.

- **Ages 7-10**: Give small allowances tied to simple chores. Introduce saving jars.

- **Ages 11-14**: Help them set savings goals, like buying a toy or a bike.

- **Ages 15-18**: Teach them to open a checking account, budget their earnings, and understand basics about credit and interest.

The goal isn't to create "perfect" financial wizards overnight. It's to build familiarity, confidence, and healthy habits.

## Step 4: Model Emotional Wisdom About Money

Money stirs up powerful emotions, pride, fear, joy, anger, often all at once. Teaching your children emotional intelligence about money is just as crucial as teaching them how to add up dollars and cents. It's not just about numbers; it's about helping them understand that emotions around money are normal, and showing them how to navigate those feelings with confidence and resilience.

- Celebrate wins without tying them to self-worth.

- Talk openly about mistakes as learning moments, not failures.

- Emphasize gratitude and generosity alongside savings and earning.

Show them that money is a resource, not a ruler of their happiness or their value.

Take a moment to celebrate out loud when you hit a goal, even a small one. You might say, "I'm really proud that I saved enough to pay this bill early!" Show them that progress is worth acknowledging. And when mistakes happen, because they will, normalize them too. You could share, "I overspent a little this week, but that's okay. I'm adjusting my plan and moving forward." By openly celebrating wins and handling setbacks with grace, you teach your children that money isn't about being perfect. It's about growth, learning, and resilience.

## Step 5: Empower Dreams

Teach your children that wealth is not only about survival, it's about opportunity.

- Encourage them to dream about businesses they could start.

- Talk about education as an investment, not just a cost.

- Help them see saving as self-love, not self-denial.

You are raising future adults who can choose boldly, live wisely, and give generously, because they saw those values in you.

## Emotional Shifts That Matter

It's natural to worry sometimes that we might be "messing up" our kids when it comes to money. After all, many of us are still carrying and healing from our own money wounds, the struggles and fears we grew up with.

But the very fact that you're here, reading these words and thinking about the kind of legacy you want to leave, is proof that you are already breaking old cycles. You are doing the brave, intentional work of creating something better.

You are already doing what so many generations before you didn't know how to do:

- Teaching with compassion, not fear.

- Leading with courage, not dread.

- Building with hope, not scarcity.

Your children don't need you to be perfect.

Your children don't need you to have all the answers. What they need most is to see you trying, learning, and growing right in front of them. Every time you take a brave step forward, even when it's imperfect, you are teaching them what resilience looks like.

Those lessons won't stop with them. They will ripple forward, shaping the way your children move through their own lives, and even how they one day teach their own children.

You are not just teaching them how to manage money.

You are rewriting the story.

Imagine a future where your children pass down lessons not built on fear, but rooted in freedom, where money is seen as a tool for possibility, not a source of strain.

**You are teaching them how to build lives anchored in power, choice, and joy.**

Let's keep building.

# How to Future-Proof Your Financial Freedom

Reaching financial stability is no small feat, especially when you've had to fight for every inch of ground you now stand on. You've broken cycles, conquered deep fears, and built strong systems to protect yourself and your family.

And yet, maybe deep down, a new fear whispers: ***What if I lose it all again?***

After fighting so hard to build your freedom, the thought of losing it can feel like a shadow lurking at the edges of your peace. It might creep in during quiet moments, tugging at your sense of security. But here's the empowering truth: you can't control every twist life may throw at you, but you can absolutely build a life that bends without breaking.

You can future-proof your financial freedom.

Let's talk about how.

## Step 1: Keep a Crisis-Ready Mindset (Without Living in Fear)

Life has a way of surprising us when we least expect it. The goal isn't to somehow avoid every storm; it's to build a shelter strong enough to weather anything that comes.

Your Emergency Fund is your first layer of protection, your financial safety net. But just as important is your emotional readiness: the steady mindset that reminds you, even in the face of uncertainty, that you are prepared, capable, and strong.

Ask yourself:

- If my income dropped tomorrow, what steps would I take?

- If an unexpected expense hit, which budget categories could flex?

- Who is in my emotional support circle if I need advice or encouragement?

Write your answers down. Knowing your "battle plan" ahead of time brings confidence, and confidence calms fear.

Future-proofing means acknowledging that challenges will come, but believing, deep down, that they don't have the power to undo everything you've built. It's knowing you are strong enough to bend without breaking, and resilient enough to keep moving forward no matter what life throws your way.

## Step 2: Schedule Annual Financial Checkups

Just like your physical health needs regular checkups, your financial health does too. Think of it as part of caring for your future self.

Once a year, choose a day and mark it clearly on your calendar, your "Financial Health Day." Treat it with the same importance you would a birthday or a holiday. Block off the time, honor it, and use it to check in with your goals, your habits, and your dreams.

During your Financial Health Day:

- Review your savings, debt, and investments.

- Update your budget for any life changes.

- Check insurance policies and beneficiaries.

- Reflect on what went well financially and what you want to improve.

This isn't a time for judgment, only honesty, reflection, and gentle adjustments. Your annual checkup is your chance to honor the ground you've gained, fine-tune what needs a little care, and celebrate the wins that might have quietly slipped past you otherwise.

Future-proofing your finances isn't about obsessing over every tiny detail or living in fear of what could go wrong. It's about staying connected to your money with confidence, clarity, and pride. It's about making the conscious choice to engage with your finances from a place of strength and hope, not from panic or fear.

## Step 3: Always Keep a "Growth Plan"

Financial freedom isn't a destination you reach once and for all, it's a flowing, evolving journey. Like a river, it keeps moving, shifting, and changing with you as you grow and move through different seasons of life.

Keep growing by:

- Learning new skills that can increase your income.

- Staying curious about investments and passive income

options.

- Challenging yourself to dream bigger every year.

Maybe you'll start a side business. Maybe you'll move into a higher-paying career. Maybe you'll invest in real estate. The point is: **keep expanding your options.**

When we stop growing, we start to weaken the very foundation that keeps our financial freedom strong. True security isn't found in standing still, it's found in continuously challenging ourselves to learn new skills, explore new opportunities, and stretch into new dreams. Growth isn't just about chasing bigger ambitions; it's about making sure the life you are building stays resilient, flexible, and prepared for whatever the future may hold.

Picture this: Five years from now, you're sitting at your kitchen table, the morning sun spilling through the windows, a cup of coffee warm in your hands. You realize something powerful, emergencies no longer send you scrambling. You don't flinch at unexpected expenses. You're steady, calm, ready. You're thriving.

You sip your coffee slowly, without anxiety buzzing beneath the surface. You dream up vacations without guilt clouding the excitement. You breathe deeply and freely, knowing with full certainty, you built this peace.

## Step 4: Teach Financial Resilience to Your Children

You've already begun teaching your children the basics of money management. Now, take it one step further: teach them resilience.

- Normalize talking about both wins and setbacks.

- Model how to adjust when life changes without panic.

- Celebrate smart pivots as much as big successes.

Show them that true wealth isn't about living a life free from hardships. It's about meeting those challenges with wisdom, grace, and unwavering determination.

When you teach your children resilience, through your words, your actions, and your steady belief in growth, you aren't just protecting your own future. You're building a foundation of strength and good decision making that will echo through generations to come.

## Step 5: Surround Yourself with Financial Positivity

The people and messages you surround yourself with have a powerful influence on your mindset, your confidence, and your future. The voices you listen to most often will shape how you see yourself and what you believe is possible. Choose them wisely.

Protect your mindset by filling your world with:

- Financial education podcasts.

- Books by women who have built wealth and resilience.

- Communities of single mothers, entrepreneurs, and builders who share tools, hope, and encouragement.

When challenges come, those positive influences will remind you who you are: **powerful, prepared, and capable.**

## Emotional Shifts That Matter

Future-proofing your life isn't about living in fear of what might go wrong. It's about honoring yourself enough to build thoughtfully, plan with bravery, and stay flexible through whatever comes your way.

It's about stepping into your full power, trusting that while storms may still roll in, you are no longer standing defenseless in the open. You have already built your shelter. You have already laid the steady ground beneath your feet. You're not at the mercy of change anymore; you are shaping your future with wisdom, courage, and resilience.

Imagine yourself standing tall right where you are, feeling the quiet strength you have earned. Let this sink in: you are living the future you once could only hope for.

You didn't fight so hard to reach stability just to live in fear of losing it. You didn't come all this way just to get by. You came this far to rise, to dream bigger, to stand stronger, and to build a life so deeply grounded in your own strength that even the fiercest storms can't shake it.

Everything you need to create the life you deserve is already inside you.

Let's keep building that future, one powerful brick at a time.

Thank you for reading. If you enjoyed this book, or found it helpful, please take a moment to leave a review with the retailer where the book was published. As a new author, a review means everything!

# Bonus Chapter: Emergency Grace Plans

## Preparing for Setbacks Without Losing Hope

There's something nobody likes to talk about when it comes to building a better life:

**Setbacks happen.**

You can plan carefully. You can budget, save, invest, and stay motivated. And still, life has a way of throwing curve-balls, an unexpected bill, a job loss, a medical emergency, or a moment that rattles the ground beneath you. No matter how prepared you are, unexpected challenges are part of the journey.

**And when that happens, it's not proof that you failed.**

It's proof that you're living a real life.

The real difference between staying trapped in survival mode and rising stronger after setbacks isn't luck or perfection, it's having a plan for grace. It's having a way to catch yourself gently when life doesn't go according to script.

Today, we're going to talk about how to build an Emergency Grace Plan, a practical and emotional toolkit to help you weather storms without losing hope or momentum.

## Why You Need a Grace Plan (Not Just an Emergency Fund)

We've already talked about the importance of having an emergency fund, because it's that crucial. Having money set aside for unexpected events isn't just a safety net; it's often the difference between weathering a storm and getting pulled under by it.

But here's the thing: an emergency fund is just money. It's a financial tool. It can't talk you down from a spiral. It can't help you silence the despair that can creep in when life blindsides you.

A Grace Plan is more than a savings account. It's your emotional safety net for hard times. It's a simple, intentional guide you create for yourself in calm moments, so that when life feels overwhelming, you have something steady to lean on.

A Grace Plan is a combination of emotional self-care, prepared strategies, and mindset shifts. It's the way you agree to treat yourself when things get hard, with kindness, clarity, and patience, instead of spiraling into despair, panic, or fear.

Without a Grace Plan, emergencies often trigger panic reactions. When despair takes over, it can lead to impulse spending, abandoning your long-term financial goals, spiraling into shame and self-blame, or even giving up altogether. Sometimes, the emotional aftermath does more damage than the emergency itself.

But with a Grace Plan in place, you equip yourself to respond thoughtfully instead of reacting in fear. You move through setbacks with resilience, self-compassion, and a clear, loving path back toward your dreams.

Let's walk through how to build your own Grace Plan, a plan that doesn't just protect your bank account, but also safeguards your hope, your dignity, and your future.

## Step 1: Create a "Grace Fund"

**Yes, you still need cash.**

But think of it differently. Your Grace Fund isn't a separate savings account from the emergency fund we discussed earlier.

It's part of the same journey. It's the first milestone: a small, reachable starting point that gives you options and breathing room while you continue building toward a larger emergency fund. It's about creating a first layer of security, not preparing for doomsday.

Start with a mini-goal:

- **First Goal:** $500 set aside for true emergencies

- **Next Goal:** One month of bare-bones living expenses

- **Stretch Goal:** 3–6 months of living expenses

And if that feels impossible right now? **Breathe.**

Even saving $5 a week is an act of resistance against chaos. It's a promise to your future self that you're worth protecting.

## Step 2: Draft Your "Emergency Response Scripts"

When stress levels rise, clear thinking becomes harder. Emotions can cloud your judgment, making even small decisions feel overwhelming. That's why preparing a simple, thoughtful plan ahead of time is so powerful. It gives you something steady to lean on when your mind feels scattered.

Prepare simple scripts you can use when emergencies hit:

- **For Yourself:** "I am allowed to pause and think before acting."

- **For Family/Friends:** "I'm handling some unexpected expenses right now. I can't commit to anything extra."

- **For Your Employer:** "I'm managing a personal emergency and will update you as soon as I can."

Having these ready helps you respond thoughtfully instead of reactively, protecting your finances and your mental health.

## Step 3: Identify Your "Grace Support Team"

You don't have to carry the weight of emergencies by yourself. Support is part of the plan, not a last resort.

Make a list of safe people you can reach out to for different types of support:

- Emotional (someone who listens without judgment)

- Practical (someone who can watch kids, lend a car, brainstorm options)

- Financial (if possible, someone who could offer a small loan, with clear terms, if absolutely necessary)

Knowing who you can call *before* you need them lowers panic and helps you make empowered choices.

**Real-Life Snapshot:**

When Olivia, a single mom raising her daughter on her own, was hit with a sudden ER visit, the panic hit hard at first. But because she had taken the time to build her Grace Support Team in advance, she wasn't left to navigate it alone. She called her t friend Janie to watch her daughter, leaned on her church community for emotional support, and used the small emergency fund she had set aside to cover co-pays. Instead of spiraling into fear and chaos, Olivia moved through the storm with courage and clarity, staying grounded in her long-term goals and protecting the future she was working so hard to build.

## Step 4: Set Your "Grace Mindset Rules"

Emergencies can easily trigger shame spirals, making you feel like you've failed or lost ground. Instead of letting those emotions take over, you can meet them head-on by setting personal "rules of grace" ahead of time, simple reminders that help you stay grounded, compassionate with yourself, and focused on moving forward:

- **No Beating Yourself Up:** Emergencies happen to everyone.

- **No All-Or-Nothing Thinking:** One setback doesn't erase all your progress.

- **No Isolation:** Reach out. Tell someone. Ask for help.

- **No Financial Self-Sabotage:** Pause before making big money decisions under stress.

You are still a capable, powerful builder of your future, even when you're in survival mode.

## Step 5: Create Your "Return Map"

Having a comeback plan in place can shorten your recovery time and help you regain your footing more quickly when life throws you off track. It gives you a clear, gentle path back toward stability, even when everything feels chaotic.

Create a simple Return Map:

**Example Return Map:**

When Samantha unexpectedly lost her job, fear and uncertainty hit hard, but she didn't let them take over. She leaned into the Grace Plan she had built for moments like this. First, she paused every non-essential expense, giving herself breathing room to think clearly. Then she applied for local aid programs to stabilize her housing situation. After that, she shifted her budget into bare-bones mode, while she searched for a new job. After successfully finding a new source of income, Samantha chose a tiny but powerful goal: to rebuild $200 in her Grace Fund within 90 days. By focusing on small, steady actions, Samantha kept herself grounded. She moved through the chaos one brave, imperfect step at a time, proving that setbacks don't define her; how she rises through them does.

- **First Step:** Stabilize immediate needs (housing, food, utilities).

- **Second Step:** Reassess your budget, realign based on new realities.

- **Third Step:** Choose one small financial goal to rebuild momentum (ex: rebuild Grace Fund).

- **Fourth Step:** Celebrate tiny wins aggressively.

**You don't have to fix everything at once. You just have to start steering the ship again.**

## Emotional Shifts That Matter

Needing a Grace Plan doesn't make you weak. It doesn't make you irresponsible. It doesn't mean you failed. It means you are courageous enough to prepare for the real, messy, beautiful life that you are living, not some fantasy where nothing ever goes wrong.

It means you understand that true resilience isn't about pretending storms won't come, it's about learning how to dance in the rain. It means you are wise enough to know that setbacks are part of growth, not a sign you are broken. It means you are powerful, because you choose hope over despair every single time.

You are not starting over. You are moving forward, carrying every hard-earned lesson, every ounce of resilience, and every fierce, still-burning dream with you.

Take a deep breath. Feel the weight of your strength, not the burden of mistakes, but the solid, unshakeable foundation you have built by surviving, adapting, and continuing to believe in what's possible.

**You are starting forward.**

Let's keep building.

# Conclusion
## You Are the Wealth. You Are the Legacy.

Take a deep breath and look back at how far you've come. You didn't just skim words on a page; you showed up for yourself in ways you once thought might be impossible. You faced fears that tried to bury you. You challenged the old stories you were handed; about what you could have, who you could become. And, step by imperfect step, you started laying down something brand new, a foundation built not from scarcity or shame, but from hope, strength, and purpose.

Maybe when you first began this journey, the dream of real financial peace felt so far away it almost hurt. Maybe there were nights when you questioned if all the effort would ever add up to anything more than just survival. Maybe you doubted if someone like you could ever claim lasting freedom.

But look at you now. Still standing. Still rising. Still choosing to believe in the woman you are becoming.

And now you know the truth: wealth isn't some far-off finish line reserved for the lucky few. It's built here, in the small, ordinary moments you live every day, in every dollar you protect with care, in every brave boundary you set to honor your future, and in every tiny new belief you dare to plant deep in your own heart. Wealth grows quietly, choice by choice, right where you stand.

Wealth begins with you, not just the money you hold in your hands, but the strength you've cultivated deep inside your soul. You are creating the blueprint your children will one day follow, not because you lived every moment perfectly, but because you chose to live bravely. Every small decision you make today is a love letter to the woman you are becoming and to the family you are leading toward a freer, stronger, more beautiful future. There will still be hard days. Life will still throw its curve-balls. But now, you have built the resilience to meet them head-on.

But here's what matters most: you are not the same woman who first picked up this book. You are a woman who now protects her peace fiercely, who honors her dreams even when no one else sees them, and who builds freedom one courageous, messy, ordinary choice at a time. Even when it feels painfully slow. Even when it feels invisible. Even when the world isn't clapping or even noticing, your progress matters. Your growth matters.

You matter.

If you remember nothing else, let it be this: you are not standing still, waiting for your future to begin. You are already building it, with your hands, your choices, and your heart. So pause for a moment. Place your hand over your chest, feel the strength beating there, and say it out loud, just for you:

"I am the wealth. I am the legacy."

Let those words sink into your bones. Because Brave Money isn't about waiting for permission from the world. It's about recognizing you have already granted it to yourself. It's about showing persistence when quitting would be easier. It's about holding onto patience when results feel slow. It's about protecting your peace fiercely and celebrating every hard-won step forward.

You are the architect of your future, building not just wealth in your bank account, but also in your spirit, your story, and your family's legacy. And when fear inevitably comes knocking, because it will, you'll have something stronger to lean on. You'll remember: you are not broken, you are becoming. You are not behind, you are rising. You are not just surviving, you are leading a legacy that will echo far beyond today.

When doubt creeps in, whispering that you're too late, too tired, or too far gone, you'll know the truth: you are already proof. Every dollar you protect, every boundary you honor, every small, stubborn dream you refuse to give up on, you are living it. You are Brave Money in motion.

And Brave Money women?

We don't just survive.

We rise.

We build.

We soar.

Imagine this: five years from today, you sit at your kitchen table, coffee in hand, sunlight streaming through the windows. Your emergency fund is strong. Your goals are thriving. Your children watch you living a life you once only dreamed about, and they're learning, by your example, that freedom is possible because you showed them how. You say yes to opportunities without hesitation now, breathing deeply, not with anxiety gripping your chest, but with quiet, steady gratitude. You smile because you know, deep in your bones, that you built this life, brick by brick, step by step, choice by brave, stubborn, beautiful choice. And the future you once thought was so far away? It isn't living somewhere out of reach. It's already here, unfolding through the courage you've shown, one powerful moment at a time.

## *The Brave Money Manifesto*

*I honor progress over perfection.*

*I choose hope over fear.*

*I build boundaries that protect my peace.*

*I celebrate every win, no matter how small.*

*I believe in my ability to create wealth and freedom.*

*I refuse to measure my worth by my bank balance.*

*I lead with courage, even when I'm scared.*

*I am the author of my financial story.*

*I am the builder of my legacy.*

*I am Brave Money in action.*

You have already become this woman, the one who dreams boldly, who builds fiercely, and who lives beautifully without apology. You have always been becoming her, even when you couldn't yet see it. So let's keep building, with courage in your chest and hope in your hands. Your future isn't some far-off dream; it's unfolding right now, piece by piece, with every brave step you take.

And it's even braver, stronger, and more beautiful than you can imagine.

# About the author

Sefi Wells is a passionate advocate for single mothers, financial empowerment, and the belief that no woman should ever feel trapped by her circumstances.

Sefi Wells writes for the woman who carries the world on her shoulders and still dares to dream of something more.

A mother, creator, and advocate for emotional resilience, Sefi knows firsthand the journey from burnout to hope. Her writing offers a lifeline to single mothers who are ready to heal, to breathe again, and to rebuild a life that feels like their own.

She believes deeply that every woman has the power to rise, to rebuild, and to thrive, no matter where her journey begins.

**This book is a celebration of that power. And it's only the beginning.**

# Also by

**Also by Sefi Wells**

**The Brave Rebuild Series**

- **Resilient Heartbeats** *A Healing Guide for Single Moms to Overcome Burnout, Stay Motivated, and Find Joy Again* (An empowering roadmap for emotional healing, resilience, and self-renewal.)

- **Brave Money** (This book) *Build Financial Freedom, Confidence, and Wealth as a Single Mom, Without Shame, Guilt, or Fear* (A bold guide to financial empowerment, rebuilding confidence, and claiming your freedom.)

www.ingramcontent.com/pod-product-compliance
Lightning Source LLC
Chambersburg PA
CBHW071007120626
46546CB00003B/978